101 *Mandalas*

Amazing Patterns
Adult Coloring Book

Alex Svain

This is a great product for anyone who enjoys adult coloring books or adult coloring pages. Adult coloring books are a great anxiety aid and stress-relieving activity, and the repetition of these mandalas will help you to relax while you color.

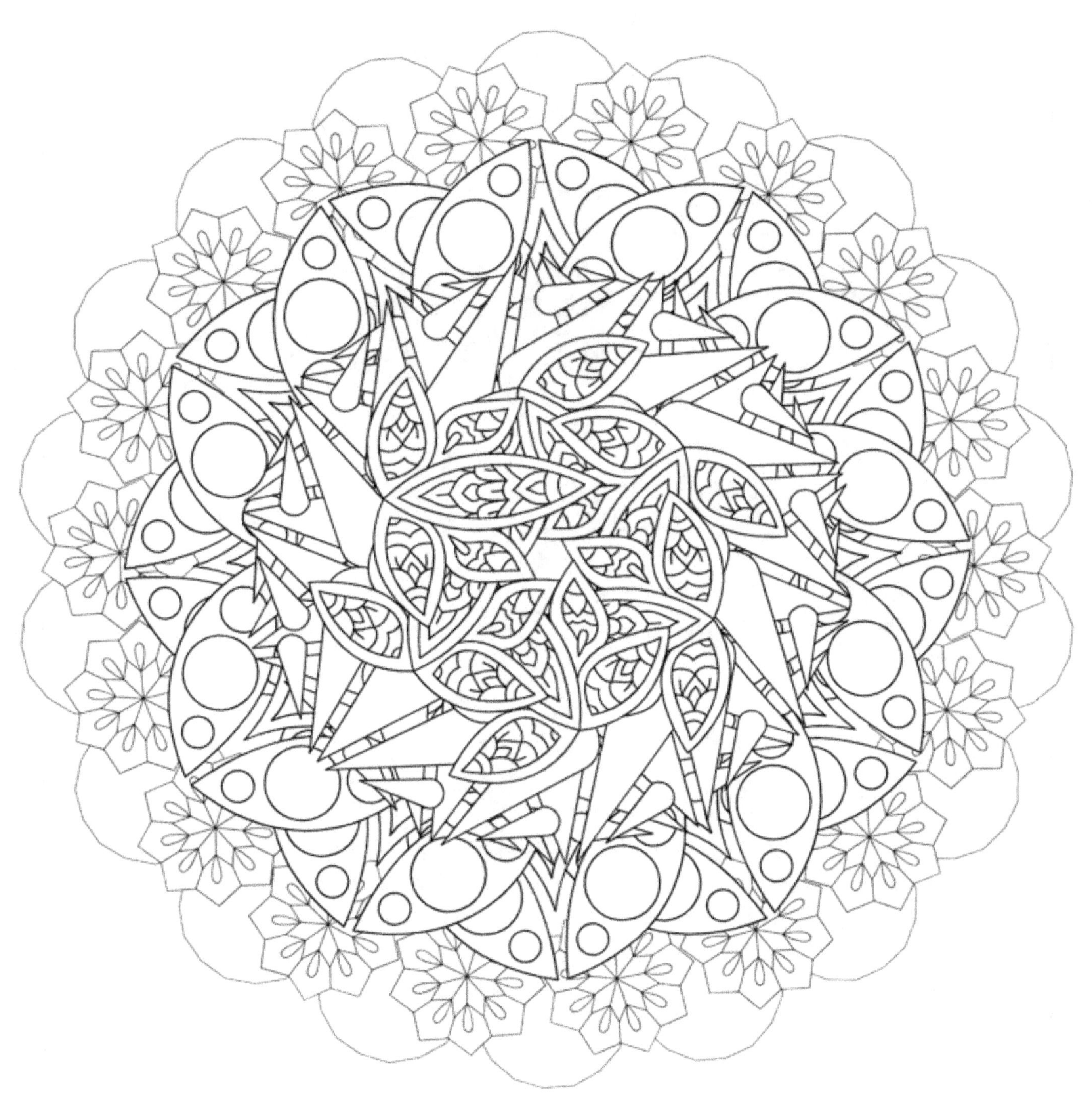

www.ingramcontent.com/pod-product-compliance
Lightning Source LLC
Chambersburg PA
CBHW081303250726
48662CB00008B/2374